THE BOY WHO READS IN THE TREES

Also by Ron Mohring:

Survivable World

The Boy Who Reads in the Trees

Ron Mohring

THE WORD WORKS
WASHINGTON, D.C.

THE WORD WORKS
P.O. Box 42164
Washington, DC 20015
editor@wordworksbooks.org
Author photograph: Randy Barlow
Interior design: Emma Berver
Cover design: Susan Pearce
Cover art: Angie Reed Garner

ISBN: 978-1-944585-66-2
LCCN: 2023941913

Acknowledgments

My deepest thanks to the readers and editors of the following journals in which these poems first appeared, sometimes in earlier versions:

Assaracus: "All Afternoon," "It Was Nothing," "Late Testament"
Bloom: "The Sound"
Connecticut River Review: "Holding On"
Evergreen Chronicles: "Late Poem for My Sister"
5 A.M.: "Running Away but Not Too Far" as "In Waves"
The Gettysburg Review: "The Real Story"
Glass: A Journal of Poetry: "The Surrogate"
Impossible Archetype: "Peas, Again"
The James White Review: "The Culvert"
Lodestar Quarterly: "Invisibility"
The Louisville Review: "The Humpbacked Trunk"
Mangrove: "Fire," "Torture"
MAYDAY: "Spiral"
Mollyhouse: "Bramble"
The Night Heron Barks: "Trinkets for a Shaman's Necklace"
North Dakota Quarterly: "Penny Candy"
phoebe: "Hair"
Porcupine Literary: "The Daughter's Body"
qarrtsiluni: "Sleepers"
Ran Off with the Star Bassoon: "Lemon Seed Sister"
Under a Warm Green Linden: "Soap"

"Hair" was featured on PoetrySuperhighway.com and was reprinted in *Assaracus 14: Joy Exhaustible* (Sibling Rivalry Press, 2014).

Some of the poems in this book previously appeared in *Touch Me Not*, a limited-edition chapbook from Two Rivers Review Press; and in the chapbook *Relative Hearts* (Lily Poetry Review).

"Go" and "It Was Nothing" appeared in *Catches & Stays*, a limited-edition chapbook, in 2022.

I am in deep gratitude to the following persons, whose support and encouragement buoyed me through the long years of working on this book: Ed Madden, Mark Ward, Rogan Kelly, Robin Becker, Jeff Oaks, David J. Bauman, RJ Gibson, Liz Ahl, Bryan Borland, Seth Pennington, Boyer Rickel, Dan Vera, Julie Enszer, Christina Pacosz, Philip F. Clark. Thank you to the Stadler Center for Poetry for the recognition, camaraderie, and support I needed to gain my footing: Deirdre O'Connor, Peg Cronin, Steve Styers, Cynthia Hogue, Shara McCallum, Andrew Ciotola, Katie Hays. Thank you to my mentors at Vermont College of Fine Arts, whose work continues to inspire me: Betsy Sholl, Mark Cox, Mary Ruefle, Nancy Eimers, David Wojahn. Thank you to Karen Jaquish, Jerry Judge, and the Cincinnati Writers League Poets. Thank you to Steve Bellin-Oka and Josh Davis, my Zoom comrades. Deepest gratitude to Jan Beatty and James Allen Hall for their close attention to my work—your words have buoyed me. And finally, to Nancy White and everyone at The Word Works, thanks for inviting me to the dance again.

CONTENTS

for Lillian, and for Paul

I.

These are the days that must happen to you

Torture

Wait in the car, she says, *and lock*
the doors. We pack inside, sticky candies
in a crushed box. Thirsty. Our bare legs
pasting together, imprinted by the itchy
stitching. My finger probes the ripped seat,
rubs the dried-out cushion inside. The yellow
foam crumbles at my touch. Like an inchworm,
Mark wriggles over the back, plops
into the driver's seat, accidentally knocks the horn.
We freeze, cower. Of all things this is the most
forbidden. Tinted reflective blue, the bank windows
gaze back, coolly blank. She's taking her time,
he says, his lanky voice dry, laconic,
relentless in the wavy heat. She's gone out the back.
I squirm around to look out the rear window.
There's a robber inside, he's locking them all
in the vault, they're going to suffocate. I think
of the food in the trunk: even now it might
be starting to spoil. I'll have to drive us home,
Mark says. My eyelids are red when I close them;
it's from the blood inside. The window's too hot
to touch. I count the dried, dead bees.

The Real Story

All his life Russell's recounted stories
from the rocking chair. A gravelly soft
voice addressing the room, not singling out
a particular listener, least of all
his wife. Anna always whined her story

loudest. What a visitor recalled was
sound, not substance, the content forgotten.
Tonight Russell glows in the hospital
bed. Attended by children, grandchildren,
he winds through the best of his repertoire:
the vacant lot he planted with potatoes,

the man in the Model A he ran off
a one-lane bridge. The stories unstringing
randomly, half-finished, some doubling back.
Where's he think he's gone to? What's he telling?
She thrusts herself among them, tries to block

his fevered monologue. They ignore her.
Stay fixed on him. He's sailing toward
the darkness on a steady stream of words.
She is pushed aside like the pillows piled
in the corner, the brass fern stand they shoved
into the hall to clear space for the bed.

His face shines with sweat, his white shock of hair
is damp. His eyes in their blue sockets burn
through the shuttered room, focus suddenly
on her. He tries to pull himself up. *You.*
He spits the word as though it were a curse,

grips the bedrail, works his mouth: *Where were you?*
Anna flinches, shifts her eyes. She murmurs,

He don't mean anything. He don't know what
he's saying, now Russell you stop right now.
She is afraid. Something is happening,
something as deep as their seventy years

together, something is about to be
revealed. She backs against the doorway, thick
ankles stuffed like sausages into her
terry slippers, waits for his words to pelt
like eggs against her, spilling it all out.

INVISIBILITY

Ronnie's high in the white pine. Not the one
the wind messed up, twisting off the top that day
they all ran to the basement. The other,
taller one. Ann cried about Snowball.
Dogs know what to do in a storm, _____ said,
but Ronnie knew being chained to a tree

couldn't help. He's way higher than before.
He's brought an old garden book, the pictures
black-and-white. He likes to read the old-
fashioned names aloud, an incantation: *Moss
rose, spider flower. Snow-in-summer.* _____ says
he'll cut the damaged tree. Two years
and sap still bubbles from the jagged top. Not
yellow, not amber like he expected, but more
clear. It smells like turpentine. Imagine a wasp

getting its foot stuck: would it pull off
its own leg? *Love-lies-bleeding. Squill.*
_____'s in the back yard, laying bricks
for a grill. Ann is filling the big wheelbarrow
with water from the hose. _____ rips a black-
and-yellow bag of concrete mix and dumps it in;
gray dust flies up. Once he painted his whole hand

with Elmer's glue, held still while it dried.
He wanted a kind of glove of himself. He couldn't
get his hand out: it fixed in place like a statue.
He had to slit the back and peel it off. *Snail vine.*
Cross vine. Sky vine. He knows the climbers

by heart. *Honeysuckle. Trumpet creeper. Boston ivy,*
English ivy, Carolina jessamine. Some wrap around,
some put out sticky feet. *Blackeyed Susan vine.*
          's yanking a hoe through the gray muck;
water slurps into the dry spots, turns them dark.
Clematis, morning glory. Ronnie holds out his arms.
Grape. Kudzu. Closes his eyes. *Moonflower. Cover me.*

HER DAY JOB

The kind of general store you never see
these days. Butcher paper on a heavy rack.
Meat slicer. Enormous soda cooler. Cans
on high shelves she used a hooked pole
to reach. Magazines in wooden racks, papers
blurting *LIZ, MALCOLM, LBJ.* Candy
in the candy case, arrayed in amber
pressed glass bowls. A table where I read
every comic book. For Aquaman I practiced
holding my breath. The giant brass register
would pop pennants up when she punched
its round buttons. There was a kitchen
curtained from the main store. A sink, a stove,
a square oak rocker where she'd rest, ask me
to wake her if a customer came in. She'd lose
consciousness almost at once—her head
lolled like a broken-necked doll, she'd lightly
snore—and I'd worry and watch, hoping no one
jangled the sleigh bells nailed to the door, wanting
the quiet afternoon to last, to blanket us
against the needs of the world.

FIRE

Mark said if we ever had one we'd tie the sheets, go out
the window, but I knew I couldn't even manage the thick
gym rope. Our second floor room was a deathtrap.
The house pitched into a steep slope. I'd tie my G.I. Joe
to a spool, lean over the sill to thread him down. He'd pivot

on the lifeline cinching his waist, bounce and scrape the bricks
like the jumpers in *The Towering Inferno* who leapt to escape
the insatiable fire. It wasn't the height that scared me,
but the sheer unscaleable drop. I had no trouble climbing trees:
each branch a kind of stairstep, a pattern I'd follow

up, and up I'd go. Once _____ caught me dropping dirt
clods from high in the maple and yelled for me to get down.
When he could touch my leg he yanked me to the ground,
screaming Dammit haven't I told you you could get hurt?

Hair

There is a house painted white. There is a tree,
its trunk painted the same white. There is a dog on a chain
tangled around the tree. There is a yard but it is all dirt,

worn smooth by the dog and the girl. The girl kneels
in the dirt, singing. She is washing doll clothes in a bucket.
Stuck in the fence beside her are the dolls, their pink

scrubbed bodies drying. Their heads poked through
the chainlink fence. Hanging by their hair, little Absaloms,
little Barbies, little perfect feet. She holds one doll

under the water. Promise you won't tell, she sings,
and I'll let you go. She squeezes the doll in her fist;
little bubbles leak from its neck. Promise. Hurry up.

The Surrogate

There were no small sorrows then,
only children too small to contain them.

But he taught me to read and write.

A kind of sanctuary, you say, and I can't
disagree. Home-not-home. Sweetened poison.

The intercom. His two-note whistle,
checking in. The lock button kept
the channel open.

In the photo you are five, maybe four.
It had already started.
I remember those red sweaters.

On the back porch he whistled twice
then shushed me: *Listen!*

Nothing at first, then the same notes
in the trees,

the scarlet flash of cardinals
swooping low, dropping to the steps
for flung seed.

Their black masks never slipping.

THE CULVERT

A round mouth in the hill. Ice hangs
from the upper rim, thrusts out its flat
frozen tongue where the creek is
deepest, where a boy from school
drowned one summer, where my brother
leads. I follow as I have always
followed, inching across the terrible ice
as he rushes ahead. I fear the black
water beneath us. I know if I fall through
he will leave and not look back.

The sloped wall is rough against my hand.
I work along its dark length. At the far end
my brother slides into the dazzling light,
his body lanky, taut, entirely his own. He spins
and rushes past—I barely skip aside—
his shouts bounce through the tunnel. He stops
and jumps, jumps again and the ice cracks,
I hear it, once more and it breaks, dark water
sloshes over the broken edge, wets his shoes.
He has moved ahead, stomping, snapping
jagged pieces that slip beneath the shelf that's left.
He turns and laughs—*Come on,* he shouts,
and I know I have to move, I'm going to die,
if it's going to happen, it's going to happen now.

Penny Candy

1.

All afternoon at school I wiggled the loose back tooth,
savored its give against my tongue. Home, locked
in the bathroom, tiptoed at the mirror, I fingered
the tooth, lifting it to see the new one
breaking through a hinge of gum. A hard white bud,
the strongest bone. I don't know how long
my sister had been pounding the door. It suddenly
wrenched open and _____ filled the frame,
his face an angry blur. I yanked my finger from my mouth,
felt the tooth pop free as his hand caught my jaw. I fell
against the laundry basket, spit the tooth on the tile.
Everything stopped. I couldn't hear. Then the pain
slammed home. I curled into the spilled clothes on the floor.

2.

That evening we watched television. _____ came upstairs,
handed me a paper sack: You can each take two.
The bag was filled with penny candy. I picked two mint
Green Leafs, saved them in my pocket. Dana chose
a jaw breaker and a root beer barrel. We did not connect
the two events, didn't realize that one displaced the other.
We had not learned that generosity arose from guilt,
that any act not talked about has essentially not occurred.
Secondary teeth must last a lifetime. Bones can break,
but heal strong as before. Montpelier is the capital
of Vermont. The human heart is actually a pump.
No two snowflakes ever are the same. Everything alive
will die. Oceans blanket two-thirds of the earth. Women
menstruate, then stop. How greedy we would become,
affixing explanations to each act, fumbling through memories
like unpaired socks: *This was when.* How much easier
it must have been to take whatever was parceled out,
accept our two cents' worth.

THE DAUGHTER'S BODY

Dana banks on food as her salvation,
     stuffing her ballooning body until
          no one would dare touch her

without permission. Fantastic, unstoppable,
     she expands, a dirigible filling the house.
          She inhales and bursts its seams—

bricks and glass explode as she unfolds,
     stretching, looming above trees, the county
          water tower on its spindly legs.

Tiny families gape upward,
     lined on their greenstamp lawns, their mouths
          identical rows of O's. Her shadow

a total eclipse. In his white undershirt,
     Dana's father gropes through rubble.
          Sifting porn drops lazily:

his shiny magazines, blown skyhigh,
     flutter down, leaves from some
          forbidden tree: a blurred foldout,

an unbound adolescent offering
     her ropeburned wrists, another who resists
          and begs for punishment. Her father

looks up. His mouth moves but no sound
     comes out: fat grub upturned
          by a shovel, chewing at the sudden air.

Everyone's caught on. Dana
      leaves him there. Extends her arms
            west and east, tilts her face

to the sun. Her blood sings. A bath
      would feel like heaven. With giant steps
            she strides off toward the nearest ocean.

The Humpbacked Trunk

_____ taped the picture inside the trunk
my brother and I shared. Mom stood

in the bedroom doorway, shaking her head; he was saying
Goddamn, Lillian. They're boys. He stood back

and made us look. As if he had created her himself.
She arched suggestively against a desk,

her fringed leather jacket open to reveal her breasts.
She wore a mini skirt. Her hair was blonde. What was she doing

in someone's office, dressed like that? Smoothed flat
against the trunk lid, she would fall back into place

each time it closed. This was something I should understand,
or begin to ask about. But her frank gaze

unnerved me. Who knows what my brother felt;
he was thirteen and already an alien.

One afternoon I went upstairs and locked the door.
Eased open the trunk. I wanted to unseal

her riddle. I traced the image of her body. I felt desperate,
felt nothing, and knew this was wrong. Inventing

concerned voices, I whispered: _How strange
he's always in his room._ Mark's cackle

burst from the top bunk: he'd seen it all.
I slammed the trunk. He shot

past me, whooping, headed for the kitchen.
Mom would lean against the stove, half-listening,

straining toward something missing: a flicker
of the future, the quick moth shut in the closet

ruining the coat saved for winter. How I will turn out
wrong. I leave her there, leave my brother racing,

his tennis shoes slapping the floor. In the basement
I leave our monster. I go back to save that boy

from what he will conceal: his shame. How he will grope
to understand what they expect. He sits on the trunk,

shaking, his body like a fist. I touch his shoulder.
He jerks, spins to face the empty room. *Hang on,*

I tell him. *It'll be all right.* He stares through me,
past the open door. Their laughter bounces

up the hall. *Screw them,* he says. *Just screw them all.*

BRAMBLE

Blood brothers, he says, & brings his splashy thumb
to my face. I cringe at the torn skin. Mother's
thread & needle won't mend this error. Rusty
cans & broken glass hide in these weeds. Snakes
in waiting. Barbed wire. Nails. But coming
here was my idea: the squishy *thunk* of berries
in our buckets, their purple mess on our hands
& shirts worth the scratches & welts, the tiny
claws embedded in our arms. He sucks
his thumb & grins, his bloody teeth a tiger's,
proffers it again, his voice a purr: *Your turn.*

Running Away But Not Too Far

He waits past dark in the blue rowboat. Mosquitoes
light on his bare arms, his face. He lets them drink:

    his blood feeds multitudes. The pain is small
    and quick. The boat undulates with each breath.

        He pictures ripples moving from the center.
        If he were to make a sound, it too would leave in waves.

He has been in the boat for hours. His legs ache
from not moving. He's never learned to swim.

    In the water beneath the boat are turtles
    that could sever a finger. Once

        at the edge of the pond he'd crossed
        the path of a snapper, its spiny plastron caked

with cracking mud. The turtle had reared
and hissed. The sharp beak. The gold-flecked eyes,

    irises like stars. Later he'd wondered
    how long it had lived in the pond, whether it too

        would have its throat cut, like the turtles
        his uncle caught. Blood so thick and sudden

it looked black. He'd climbed a maple to watch:
_____ paddled the boat. His uncle

    checked the hook-strung line
    stretched just below the surface.

        He'd taken his knife and slit bark
        from a branch. The white wood beneath

felt cool. The tree was alive; he knew that.
He'd lain against the branch and licked

    the place he'd peeled bare.
    In the boat he remembers this and touches

        one arm, feels the raised welts.
        He'd like to give himself completely up:

taken in tiny increments, the blood
from his body filling theirs, lifting away

    in random directions like an impossibly slow
    explosion. They will feed on him all night

        as he lies curled in the boat,
        holding himself still and wholly responsible.

It Was Nothing

Just tall enough to raise the hammer but never able
to drop it on the gaping heads of whiskered catfish,
those sad comics in their too-tight suits we had
to shuck with pliers, their beady eyes rolling in bewilderment.
Of course it wasn't, of course my neighbor knew better
than to take me fishing though I begged him, of course
the worms writhed in something other than pain,
though it looked like pain, though he said it was nothing
when the cat finned him good and blood seeped from
his wrist. Blue boat rocking on the pond, sun beating
our backs. Green heron clamped like a bundle of rags
to the half-sunken log, dragonflies lighting on our rods
then flicking off again, the care he took so natural, inevitable,
and hadn't I latched onto him, wasn't this what I wanted without
knowing it? Dazed, acquiescent, carried out of my fevered body
and into the cloaking shade of the dumbstruck trees?

Holding On

It is the autumn of discovering seeds,
that plants have engineered their own survival.
Fireweed and thistle, catalpa bean
and touch-me-not. Even poison ivy
has its berries. When I cut through the field,
seeds hitch rides on my clothing, not caring
where they go. *Any place*, says the dandelion,
releasing its soft explosion.

Thirty feet up, _____ leans
over the roof's edge, nailing tin squares
to cover small holes in the eaves.
My sister crouches behind, gripping
his ankles. He will leave one hole
uncovered, insert the garden hose duct taped
to the truck exhaust, gas the brown bats
nesting in our attic. The echo of his hammer
bounces off the stucco house, across the field.

Ann is on the roof
because she understands instructions,
knows that some things simply must be done.
Sweating in her T-shirt and overalls, staring out
at nothing, she clamps his ankles and holds on.

The bindweed in the pasture
smothers the barbed wire fence,
the tendrils wrapping tight enough to choke.
It has purple morning glory flowers. The leaves
are pale and heart-shaped. I crush the brittle pods,
cup the hard black seeds in my hand. Last year's
silvered vines have frayed, are clinging still.

Trinkets for a Shaman's Necklace

Bird skull painted blue. Red
glass bead. Arrowhead. Skeleton
key. Tiny corked bottle of water
that fell as hail one green-sky day
in Ohio. Brass pen nib stained black.
Small silk knotted drapery tassel.
Yellow poker chip. Penny flattened
on the track behind the liquor store
where you first tried to kiss a boy.
Honey locust thorn. Pink handkerchief
from your mother's bureau drawer.
Loose eyelet from a shoe. Shard
of Coke bottle glass. Acorn cap.
Cat whisker. Gold filling. Marble
with a bubble trapped inside.
Name he called you when
he shoved you down.

Shadow

"An eagle!" she cried out then clapped
her hand over her mouth as we spun
to the picture window then burst
into laughter—the ragged crow
settling like torn tar paper
in the saucer magnolia
then laughing along,
its ripsaw cackle
just one more
voice calling
her stupid.

Eagle.

Crow.

Who knows
why she saw
the one inside
the other in that
moment, with what
longing she'd conjured
from its untarnished aerie
a creature that would never
deign to descend to our level?
The hand too late to put the words
back. Our jeers sticking to her like tar.

Eat Your Peas

Goddamn boys, Mark's gonna be a juvenile delinquent
and the other one's gonna turn out a fairy. Ronnie can't even
hammer a nail, Christ I don't know why I try to teach him,
he'd rather be off with a book. The way his face fell when I said
last night in front of everybody: I found your little camp
in the woods. What's he doing out there by his self all the time?
Says he's thinking. He's soft. He's trouble. Always looking
out the window like he wants to get away, like his mom,
stupid bitch, she tries that stunt again I'll blow her head off.
Nobody runs out on me. Dropping those snotty kids
all over town, two at her brother's, two at her sister's,
dragging the baby off to her old man's house. Like I don't know
she's got nowhere else to go. I found them all. Driving home
with the girls crying in the back of the truck and the boys
good and scared right next to me, I made them promise
to never run off with their mother again. Mark didn't say
a word, that shit, but Robbie said okay real quiet when I
smacked him. Little pansy. Look at them all, shaking like
stupid rabbits around the table, and her holding her belly
and spooning out mashed potatoes. Christ I don't know why
I bring good money into this house, none of you brats
knows how to appreciate a thing. Stop staring at your plates,
you think you got it bad, if you'd have seen what I saw in Korea
you'd know how goddamned good you've got it. You don't
know shit. Shut up and eat your fucking peas.

Small Hands

Season of mischief. Season of pranks. My usual
uncertainties knotted, redoubled:

confrontations lurked at every corner,
ways to slip, be *found out*,

though I can't say I knew then what that meant.

·

Season of masks, of mutation: how the gray-barked ginkgo
simmered chrome yellow,

then dropped almost at once and without shame
its skirt of bisected leaves

I thought looked like butterflies. I strung them in clusters
with needle and thread,

was disappointed at the effect: not tassels, not magic at all.
What did I expect?

·

Season of dimming. Of turning, tunneling inward, the way the last wasps
drilled into wet fallen pears.

Shaking the tree, how we ducked and dodged the tawny bombs.
I'd gather a bagful every year,

drag it to the porch for my grandmother. Next visit she'd bring me
a jar of preserves: too sweet,

too candied, the sugar gritty on the spoon. It wasn't the pears I liked
but that she made them for me.

·

Season of death. Of questions and fear: how I flung water
at our calico, Clyde,

because her yowling kept me awake. Heavy with kittens,
she fled to the woods.

When I found her at last by the highway—the stench and bloat,
the matted fur, crushed skull—

I thought no punishment could be enough. I told no one.
I carried her wreckage

across the field, buried my secret and threw the shovel
into the creek.

·

Years later, visiting a friend

whose son had died (the tractor had pinned him
for hours), her daughter,

Aimee, led me through the woods to her brother's
secret house. A simple shed,

but with a seamless door—no handle—until she
pointed: four smooth grooves

carved to match his fingertips. I touched the worn
grain. *He had small hands,*

whispered Aimee. Then, skipping off like some tiny
nymph, sang out: *Still does!*

I stumbled after her, bereft of sense.

·

Jeans stuffed with leaves,

pillowcase body the same, my brother's old shit-kicker boots
tied with red laces

to the cuffs. Pine branches poking from flannel sleeves.
Whose old hat?

Inside a plastic bag a dented volleyball head that lolled,
wouldn't hold straight.

Strung up, the body rotated slowly for maybe five minutes
till Mom came flying

Take it down take it DOWN! She kicked the broken scarecrow
into the gully, rushed back

to grab my arm: *Never NEVER do that! If* _____
had seen . . . It's how

his father died.

•

We capped the tops on the pumpkins. The candles blackened
their flesh. Spice. Singe. Ruin.

How He Did It

BONIFAY, FL: "Ronald Mohring, of Cincinnati,
Ohio, yesterday shot his sister and her husband
before killing himself . . ."

He wanders through the living room. Nan's on the phone.
She's cooking, stirring as she talks. She lifts a steaming spoon. Her back
turned to him. He calls to her. She's laughing. Nan, he says again.

She gestures him to wait. Again, he thinks. Just let me in her room,
he says. If that's Eileen, tell her to wait. You're always on the phone—
—Will you please *wait*? she says. Turns back to the stove. Nan talks

with Eileen once a week. The talks help catch her up again.
It's Ron again, she says. He's back to wanting into Mama's room . . .
He wants me off the phone. Who knows? He never got along with her

before she died. He hated her—well, fine, not hate . . . The way he talks,
Eileen, I can't say on the phone . . . Nan glances through the door again.
*Oh God, hold on—*The living room is still. A chair shoved on its back.

The ceiling fan ripped down. Nan backs away, feels the door behind her.
He's coming back into the room. You bitch. His face dark red. He talks
as though the words could kill. Again: You bitch. She lunges for the phone

beside the stove. The phone receiver squawks. She hears the back
door opening. Gene's home again. This can't be happening to her.
Her mouth is gaping. She can't talk. Gunshots in the other room—

THE FLOOD

I scramble along an embankment clenching a covered
basket. My mother's hands thump

inside, soft as spiders. I reach a wide slurry:
rain slaps mud, a frying sound. A braid of hair
switches against the current. I step

onto a bobbing log, balancing. The braid submerges
with a wet snap. The rain stings. The log revolves,
bumps a tilted stove—its door

bangs open and my mother's legs spring out, jerking
frog spasms, steaming as they hit the water, yank
themselves away. I leap

to a stone; it gives beneath my weight. I slip and plunge,
feet snagged in the soft bottom. The stone resurfaces,
no stone: the lips

unhinge, release a string of something black. The eyelids
close. I close my own and set the basket down, release
my grip.

The current nudges, pulls, insistent, cold. When
I wake, all of her has gone.

Believe It

We drove the van all the way from Cincinnati
to Niagara Falls. Dew spangled the chilly grass;
odd black squirrels capered near our picnic
table, then vanished in the heavy fog. Like traffic,
a faint roar made me shudder: how close were we
to where the earth and water dropped? We found
a tower, rode up its outside elevator,
clinging to the bar. Looking down at the horseshoe,
the stacked plume, someone decided we ought
to ride one of the bobbing white boats. The deafening
water, the yellow slickers, the tourists gripping wet
wooden rails. The women and men locked inside barrels,
rocketing into the hole carved by the plunge. I threw up
into a bucket.
               Later we visited the Ripley's Museum:
the man who ate a bicycle piece by piece, the monks
who walked with candles stuck in sockets
drilled into their skulls, women who stitched so finely
they lost their sight. In the bathroom, a man
stepped up to the urinal next to mine, shook his cock,
kept shaking it. I felt all clammy and couldn't pee.
The door opened again: I spun around,
dashed out. There were chairs with leather straps.
There were shiny pans and instruments
for sawing bones, jewelry made from human hair.
In the lobby, a giant faucet seemed to float in midair,
gushing constant water. A trick, Ann said,
but we couldn't figure how it worked.
I remember heading up into Canada, and lakes,
and digging spruce seedlings with a butter knife.
We hid them in a plastic cooler, said nothing
when asked by the man at the border
if we'd anything to declare.

TOUCH ME NOT

He burned trash in the back field, stirring flaming paper
with a stick. Orange light leapt into the sycamore's
white limbs. The smoke choked the tree but the leaves rocked
like warming hands. He watched a blackening deodorant can,
its plastic cap melting. Waited for it to explode.

He pierced a row of eyelets along his fingertips, an even
dozen, tied red thread through each. Bloody tassels.
Little arteries tugged out and knotted. Mutant good-for-nothing
feathers. He stuck the needle into a small green pear, imagined
picking it later from the tree. The thought of it lodged in his throat.

He dripped a stolen candle on his sealed fist,
encasing it in layers. Thrust it in his pocket, imagining he lacked
the strength to break the mold.

Beside the creek, he lay down in the weeds
behind a fallen tree. Jewelweeds towered, knotty stems
like green bones. He pulled off his shirt, invited their feathery
arrival: first thin sound, then miniscule stings as mosquitoes
clouded him, pushed away laden with blood. His body
their warm metropolis. He imagined being wholly drained.

Once, with a kitchen spoon, he gouged a hole
in the dirt and then, without thinking how, pulled down
his pants and thrust his penis in. He wanted it to rain
so he could stay this way, locked to the earth. He wanted
thunder, lightning.

He found a rabbit strangled in a wire noose. He slit
a cicada to see the coil inside. He stood on the bank
and watched a moccasin slip past his feet and into the pond.
Crayfish left emptied shells in the creek, their backs

broken open. Birds ate blue-black honeysuckle
berries, and he wondered were they poison,
and how strong.

That winter, he hid in the shed. His breath fogged chrome
wrenches hanging in descending rows. He mixed them up.
Something scratched or chewed in the corner. He'd rattle
a jar of rusty nails to keep it quiet. He lay on the cold
floor and counted the pegboard holes, practiced
breathing slower, being found.

II.

Shall we stick by each other as long as we live?

Night Cook's Day Off

My new dad did his gentle best—*Respect
your tools,* for instance—to catch me up
to things I should have learned.

The sixth-grade cheerleaders wave from the fire truck
roaring past: *Mister Ron!* I graded their spelling tests
last night. Disbelief: my fingertip

clipping neatly off.

Don't look at my hand, I hiss at gaping
diners, slipping on blood I can't cup,
kicking into the kitchen toward the sink.
You asshole! screams the manager. *Look
at my floor! Why did you come through the front?*

I'd tried out back, banged the door but no

restaurant boss ever answers, unless he wants his head
blown off. Tap water spikes open the wound.
Blood on the dishes. What a splashy
disaster. I can see inside myself—

oozy meat, gray flap barely hinged—

not lost in the shiny pyracantha,
skewered on some thorn, but still with me.
Can they save it? It's this, not the blood,
that scares. Oh skin, oh flesh,
oh nerves. How I've ruined you. I wanted
to try my hand at something I loved.

Late Poem for My Sister

All evening at the round oak table we've spun our common
stories, grateful the way a family is grateful when the plane

they didn't catch has crashed, all lost in flames. We drink in
one another's faces, amazed to be here, alive and more or less

whole. Mark has told the one about the radio
_____ threw into the pond, how we circled, rowing, prodded

the bottom with a pole, hoping each clump of rising bubbles
marked its passage. We've laughed about the cake

Ann had to bake, how she gripped the mixing bowl,
raked her tongue across her teeth to work up spit

for the batter, how at supper she couldn't speak,
her tongue hurt so. We slap the table, fill our glasses

and tell another. Our monster, dead ten years,
recedes still further. And then you let it out, the story

that has curdled, the blunt revision of the history
we thought we knew: how he fixed on you, target

most desired: *This one I will break.* You hiss
the bitter words; your anger stuns. We've taught

ourselves to swathe the past with laughter—
the box is full—there's no room to hear

these accusations. Our faces burn. And what
shall I do with this sudden rage, my hands clenched

tight, what is there left to strike? My memory, rattled,
spills out a scene I'd forgotten: burning trash along the road,

some flaming ash was lifted by the wind and settled
in your hair. We danced around you, slapping at your head,

long after the spark was out, because we were children,
because it was a game, because we must have sensed

you were the easy choice. You say
we should have stopped it. You say we sent you to him,

left you behind, could have found a way if we had wanted.
You say you don't know why you're even telling this,

what it is you want. To feel somehow if not release,
then please not this sudden weight, the growing of the burden

with the telling. I want to take us back, be the one you trust,
find a way to get you out. I didn't. I didn't know.

September, 1969

Mouse dirt, Mother would mutter,
snapping the tablecloth retrieved from its moth-
bally drawer. Such tidy flecks, I couldn't
conceive of them as shit. Like the tiny harvest
corn I stacked on acorn cap platters but learned
was caterpillar poo. Behind the unfinished
garage, Brother burned his plastic soldiers,
making them more true. Black oily smoke,
dripping faces, hands transmogrified to bubbling
blobs. I dug tunnels in the damp sand
pile, loved to lie flat and snake my arm
through the cool gritty dark, fingers
erupting from cave-ins to snatch
trespassing ants. _____ was a stick I buried
over and over. A good flat stone
could be a flying car to take me anywhere.

PEAS, AGAIN

He sat on me. He held
me down. I don't remember
what I said or what set
him off, but then he was
on top of me, one hand
forcing open my mouth,
the other smacking my face.
His knees pinned back
my arms. His eyes
rolled just like Angie
Pelton's dog that day
it ate rat poison. Bootsie.
Spitting blood and foam,
staggering in the yard. Nobody
else around. I grabbed
a metal washtub off their porch
and plopped it over him,
sat on it scared to death until
he quieted. He grabbed
the bowl of peas
and shook them
in my mouth, all over
my face. I gagged and
he hit me again, threw
the bowl. It broke against
the stove. I couldn't
even hear it. I don't know
why he stopped or how
I got to live.

Size

When for the better
part of a year, Gail coaxed out shards

> —he cocks a pistol at Mom's head
> while we huddle on the porch—

I thought I was reconstructing
a monster

> —.22 rifle stock cut down to fit
> my six-year-old shoulder;
> heavy lead disc strung on wire
> before a pit he dug into the hill—

stitching horrors into a golom that would dwarf
us both

> —blue transistor radio
> snatched from the picnic table,
> thrown into the pond—

so the steel in Gail's soft voice one day

> —*I wish he could be in the room with us now;*
> *I'd have a thing or two to say to that little man*—

became the last shock to take my breath:

> —oh—

I mistook so much for power.
How large he would have seemed to any child.

Dead Letter: Pater

Of all the words you taught me not to say,
sometimes it's *love* I think I miss the most.
We played a game too dangerous to play,

and it became our life. The stupid way
you died was pure dumb luck. I want you lost
with all the words you taught me not to say,

packed in some cardboard box and filed away
with clippings saved to prove that you're a ghost.
It was a game too dangerous to play,

pushing your limits. Some kids have a way
of healing, and in time, survive the worst
of wounds. You taught me to never say

a thing unless I meant it, so today
I'm telling you: I'm finished playing host
to anger, replaying dirty tapes that say

I'm unfit. I've erased your name. Away
with you. I know that I still pay the cost
of all the words you taught me not to say:
we played a game too dangerous to play.

The Sound

I'm digging in the garden when I hear it, an inhuman grating,
a wrenching moan and I think it's an injured child and drop
my shovel and step into the street to look, the kind of sound

a dog might make in grief, my neighbor's unloading something
from his truck, the tailgate's open and there's this awful keening
as he carries boxes back and forth, it's the rusted hinges rubbing

but I can't let go of it, a sound the body would make in protest,
and I've slipped from the school bus steps, landed on my back
on the rainy pavement, everything collapses, my body buckling

and unbuckling, trying to force air back into my lungs, I stagger
up the walk like a long blackening tunnel toward the school,
my vision flickering, this horrible sound engulfing me, a human

accident, a body wreck, a wracking shuddering bass, Deena
Wintergarten pounding me on the back, screaming *He can't
breathe!* as people swirl around me, I'm parting my classmates

like a messenger with terrible news, and Neal Bannister,
the school punk, turns from his locker with a sour *I always said
that kid was queer,* and Mr. Gillison, the coach, is running

toward me as I pivot halfway up the stairs and everything
goes black and the next moment I'm in his downstairs office,
he's leaning over me, I'm listening for that sound and only then

understand it had been coming out of me, his face is close to mine,
I think of his nickname, Peachy, the boys in gym class say he can't
grow a beard, *I'm sorry,* I say, *It's not your fault,* he says, *What*

happened, he says, and I want to ask him what that other boy
was talking about, *I fell off the bus,* what did it mean, *I hit my back,*
and he helps me sit up and asks if he can lift my shirt to look,

I can't believe his hands could touch me and not hurt, but I nod,
there in the pocket of quiet surrounding us both.

Care

Once I watched my grandfather
gently untangle a climbing rose a storm
had torn from its trellis. Gloveless,

bleeding from deep scratches, he cut
with his pocketknife, removed broken
stems, setting them aside. A rose

cannot distinguish whom it inflicts.
Did it blossom because of this armor,
or despite it? Which brought forth

the other? He swiped blood from his arm
with an old shop rag then wrapped
a thorny arching stem: *Hold this here.*

Later he would show me how to save
the cuttings, stuck into quartered
potatoes and planted under pickle

jar domes. Even then I wanted
to *be* the rose, protected by his care,
yet didn't love mean harm? Was there

another kind? Together we returned
the climber to its support, though I
was little help, only there to flee

my smothering grandmother and her
doughy perfumed hugs that went on
too long. The basement he had dug

by hand was cool and dark, and once
I found an Indian head carved
from chalk. He let me take it home,

the painted features already blurring
from my touch.

SHOULDERING HIS NAME

His front tooth had a tiny pit
he'd flick with his tongue when he smiled.
Like mine, his eyes were blue. He quit

job after job, stayed, self-exiled,
plotting revenge in the basement
for years. When Mom tells the story

of how he attacked his sergeant
and got locked up, she looks away.
Imagine: pregnant, seventeen,

she's staring through a thick glass door
as he rages. She gives him one
more chance. . . I get his name, her fear.

He blows himself away. What for?
Some nights he still breathes in our ear.

That Water

I would lie in the tub, water over
my ears, lured by the sounds
underneath: the echoey *plurp!*
of each drop from the faucet,
the gritty *scrunch* when I slid even lower.
My G.I. Joe doll flexed, stranded atop
the hillock of one dry knee, desperate to hatch
a plan that might save me from going
completely under. Steam fogged
his chiseled plastic chest like the sweat
that darkened Mr. Gillison's T-shirt
in gym period. I was this close to being
lost and I knew it. I wanted Joe to swirl
to life-sized life, an unstoppered genie,
his suddenly articulate arms to lift me
from that water, his beard-flocked cheek
to nuzzle my neck: we'd make it out somehow
or else go down together.

LOCATION

It's a location joke, we used to say,
meaning you have to be there to get it.
Tonight the phrase rebounds: my brother's

phoned: *Mother's in Emergency.*
The capital invests the common word

with urgency. I ask should I come out.
He doesn't know. How to react when tests
are incomplete, when even the doctors

have questions? Though they *seem* optimistic,
he tells me, have declared satisfactory

her condition, *whatever the hell
that means.* Our conversation feels
rehearsed—it's a scene we've each

improvised before, privately
imagining the worst as if that might

fend off the possibility of real loss.
The actual and fictional unable to coexist.
We practice this theory while flying, mutter

Plane crash, plane crash, the twisted
family mantra. Though we know

this particular text by heart, we're struck
dumb, afraid we might make it real. Like a lost
prescription, like a brother's silence,

this moment waits to be filled. You have
to be there. It doesn't begin to make sense.

THE BOG

That spring the creek overflowed, rushing into the pond
where we liked to catch   and release the huge

mottled carp that flashed the surface when we'd toss
stale bread, spinning each slice   to slap the water, draw

them up. We called them goldfish, so large and heavy it took
both hands to hold them still   while someone else

worked out the hook so we could throw them back.
Deep red-orange or milky white,   often splashed

with both, though others—the ones we dismissed as *just carp*—
seemed to refuse such beauty,   their overall brown

like watered-down root beer. This was, I guessed, their
camouflage. They spawned   together in the rain,

their roiling bodies frothing the water. The pond could not
contain such commotion,   spilled over its lower lip

into the marshy bog below the hollow willow where
a mallard would hatch her brood.   She started

with nine but one by one the snappers pulled them under
until she floated alone,   regal, desolate.

Later that summer I followed a rotten odor to what was left
of the bog: a few weak puddles.   I crept out,

balancing on fallen branches. Raccoon tracks crisscrossed
the cracking mud with dainty   handprints. A puddle

seethed: tiny carp shimmied and gasped the sour water.
The stench caught in my mouth.   I ran home

to grab a pickle jar, spent all day scooping up survivors, even
as they flailed to escape   my shadow, taking me

for another predator. With each dash to the pond, I'd carry
back more water. Such awful mess.   Maybe sometimes

we're just born wrong. No one could save them all, I knew.
But how could I   not try?

Shelter

Sitting in my car a few moments before heading home because my feet
hurt after a long day, because the rain softly pitting the windshield

is a slow-scrolling pointillist watercolor, even if all the tones are gray,
even if a bank of fog obscures the river and the trashy gulls

that sail and dive the parking lot for scraps. A lulling rain.
A rain that just two weeks ago we would have cursed as snow. Cars slish past;

the cart-gatherer in his neon yellow poncho huddles under the cart corral's
awning, then, resigned, plods back out to his job. I could ease back the seat,

sleep in this rain. I'm glad we got the onions planted, though I worry
they'll rot if the weather stays cool. Everything seems off to a slow start.

I wonder where the walking man has hunkered down. Last Friday
he was near the mall, wrapped in his thick dirty coat, hauling that enormous

duffle. I've seen him sleeping roadside in a field, trudging north of here,
sometimes south, on some kind of loop, perhaps, a punished demigod

condemned to circle the fringes of our commerce. His scalded face
and unwashed hair remind me of the marsh hawk last week by the river:

clamped to a sycamore in the soaking rain, its wild, piercing gaze
separated me from anything it needed to survive.

Sleepers

Today, in Ohio, my mother
will have a small procedure.

Rejecting technicians' equivocations,
she seeks a second opinion.

Sometimes the stranger comes so close
she can almost make out his face,

but then a sound—the dog's nails
tapping the floorboards

in sleep, a branch at the window—
tugs her mind from that dream into

another, the way the Congo tetras, glinting
like silver dollars in the tank's bluish light,

shimmied suddenly from one zone
to the next, then drifted, suspended,

eyes ticking as if in thought . . . But this is not
her memory. The fish were mine. I can't

remember where they ended up. A pet store
on South Shepherd, I think, the year

we moved from Houston. Beautiful fish,
raised from small nothings. Long dorsal fins

trailing like undulant veils. Shimmer
of blue in their silver. I'd linger

to watch them hover and drift,
their bodies' slow turning, shifting

like sleepers. The world the glass contained
was like the sanctuary I imagined

my house to be: I could not enter one,
nor bear to leave the other. This phone

in my hand, the same silver
as those fish, contains, impossibly, my mother:

her voice, or its approximation,
digitally rendered. I am my mother's son.

I've always been. If there is another world
beyond this one, and if nothing I've imagined

will be there, does it not follow that somehow
we're dreaming in its belly even now?

Cusp

one hand out the window
   feel the sting
the other   on the wheel

rain throwing itself down
   they are coming
muttering   its thousand tongues

how to unbraid the spatter
   they are coming soon
this hammer-seethe   vibrating

the car like some defunct instrument
   they are coming but
whose drumming I strain to pierce

pluck pattern from this wild blur
   cannot assist you

frightened by   my own wet hand

Spiral

But what was on my partner's mind that long night I lay in the next
room, unaware we would not speak again?

·

Before the Galveston hurricane, we braced on the rain-whipped strip
of beach, squinting at leaden clouds for some pattern, some hint of spiral.

·

At twelve, forgotten, he struggled beneath the Tennessee
River, pinned upside-down, his mother oblivious, chatting on the sandbar.

·

A life in an instant. A moment expanding like oil
on water into an irrevocable stain.

·

He kicked free. Climbed out, coughing. Told no one. And took the lesson
into himself like a rusty nail to the foot: secret wound, slow poison.

·

His father entered the kitchen, waving his swollen cock at his mother,
frying eggs in lard: *You want any of this?* We stared at our plates.

·

You can't see it because you're *in* it. What's needed
is perspective. The GPS says *here,* and now, *here.* But where is next?

·

For twenty years a phrase—*climbing dim stairs*—would come unbidden to my mind. I never knew what to make of it.

·

I can't sleep in this house, I hissed. *I think that man might shoot us in our bed.* So we rented a cabin, didn't tell them where.

·

Yet his uncanny vision. As his mother died two hundred miles away, he stared at the farmers market crates emblazoned *Hazel, Hazel, Hazel.*

·

I went to work. I came home late. Even as I climbed the stairs, I knew. And then I saw. And will never unsee him there.

Go

All your meals will be in color now.
All your lights are green. You're good to go.
All your love returns a thousandfold.
All your coddled seedling trees will grow.

Almost all your geese leave in a vee.
Forget the earthbound gander pulling all
the feathers from his breast. *Time wounds all heels,*
said someone clever but unkind. It's all

forgiven now. Death wipes plates clean, flings
these leftovers at the bin, the wall, who cares?
Not you. Not now. Forget the tremor, all
that spilled from forks you tried to steady, all

the cups half-filled. We're brimming over,
wholly open now, like all your doors,
flung wide. It hurts. This light. It's everywhere
you were. And now you're there, and there, and there.

Underworld

And what did I think I was doing that evening in the driveway,

didn't I already know a live oak had lifted the concrete slab,

hadn't I only to look up to see its living presence? What made me

believe the space beneath was only that—a crack, a darkened place

to dump the bright metallic shavings from the rock tumbler's drum?

Do not put down the sink, the kit's instructions warned. I rinsed the stuff

into the crevice with the garden hose, had started to turn away when

the earth moved then blinked: two hunkered toads, their eyes flecked

gold as the silvery stuff that now coated their permeable backs . . .

They stared from their cave without rancor, oh mercy,

I watered them, till dark fell hard I flushed that home I had ruined,

praying to wash them clean.

LATE TESTAMENT

What are the birds?
Gray, gray as slate.

No, I mean what are the birds?
Little scraps of pity.

What are they doing?
Clasping too tightly.

What do they tell you?
It's already too late.

What do you answer?
My tongue is too narrow.

What does that mean?
The birds understand.

How does the tree feel?
Terribly burdened.

How do you know this?
It's not what she planned.

What are they doing?
Collecting as one thought.

What does it look like?
An animate blanket—

What does the tree feel?
This loss will be harder—

You mean when the birds go?
Yes, when the birds go.

All as one garment
　　　all in one motion

　　　they mimic the body,
its copied form flung into air—

Who could endure such a thing?

ALL AFTERNOON

I hid in the campus library with books I'd pulled
        for their titles
or the lines of a random poem inside, trailing my fingers
        along their spines,
selecting them solemnly, loving their company, how they
        waited to be found.
I had slipped away from work, from home, and where else
        to go but here,
the upper floor, the quiet corner near the abused art books,
        the wide window
facing south toward the river with its one mountain, its gulls
        flashing like windblown
scraps of paper? I read and read, copying lines and sometimes
        whole poems
into my notebook; I could do this all day and not tire of it, though
        I couldn't help
but watch the stealthy men slip up the corridor, pause to drink
        at the fountain
then glance around before entering the men's room. I counted
        the minutes
they waited; I watched them go; I could have been invisible.
        I thought this might
be how the dead must feel: to wait, brimming with longing
        but faceless,
voiceless, the way a book depends on human connection
        to become
complete, a closed circuit. Of all the furtive men that afternoon,
        just one nodded,
and though I nodded back, speechless with hunger, I understood
        I was nothing
but a witness, and the humming lighting seemed
        to seep inside
the desk's sharp edges which brightened and shook into
        a piercing wind
that filled the room and blew me hollow as a winter reed.

THE TELLING

I have no bees to tell but you.
You pause at the round threshold, pivot
your delicate, brutal face. Your body
a dark jewel, spill of molten garnet

ready to sizzle and sting. What do
you care? Should I proffer my ear,
would you resist its whorl?
This paper brain you engineer,

dangling from a single divot
glued to the wrenhouse roof—what mind
does it contain? I've watched a mantis
cooly grasp your cousin to eat

its writhing body, starting with the face.
Tell me this death means something to the world.

Dendromancy

The answer always travels slowly. Ask the boxwood
hedges, so full
last week of clicking larvae they seemed to break

into a kind of speech. Or the Rhizosphaera fungus
working its way
up the branches of the neighbor's blue spruce,

casting ruined needles down. I stare out at this half-
dead tree and can't tell
if it's raining: Trick of the light? Or just my aging eyes?

The mourning doves nest higher every year,
worrying fresh twigs
into a new accommodation. Finches clamber

and dart through their doomed home. The outcome's
inevitable—the host
consumed by the smallest guest—but even though

for now there seems a kind of impasse, the top half
churning out its green
rebellion, my god, the whole thing's hard to watch.

Soap

All this week we've heard the geese, so high
their voices seem directionless, everywhere
or nowhere. But today I spy a rangy mass
tangling and untangling, weightless knot whose strings
shift and weave in seeming disorder, the whole mass
writhing and calling, a flung tangle of loose
ends billowing, not a vee among them. I sit
in my car, windows down to better hear them,
pummeled by late February gusts, counting down
the minutes, telling myself it's nothing to be
unprepared, I can think on my feet,
the students won't smell my hesitation and turn
on me like jackals. It's nothing to feel hollow
and windblown, your confidence scrubbed raw
like filthy parking lot snow refusing to vanish,
it doesn't matter that the tenured professor next door
sneers and looks away when I greet him in the hall,
and I remember my father saying the worst, most
shameless bickering he ever faced was when
he was a teacher, my father who, one day, pulled off
his shirt and leaned in so I could see and touch
the small rectangle imbedded beneath the skin
of his left pectoral: *Isn't that amazing*, he said softly.
It was the size of a bar of hotel soap. It gave us
eight more years with him. The geese have gone
upriver; now it's just the wind. My dear father who daily
sank into his chair like an astronaut preparing
for departure, loving this earth he knew he would
be leaving. What of anything I have to do today
could ever be so hard?

DIFFICULTY

Mother in the restaurant seems almost angry, a near-state
that I sense more often lately, like a kettle never
hot enough to shriek. She's always in this *readiness*
for conflict, as if she must defend her own interests
against every single person here. I worry

for her soul. She's 80 now, has honed her knack for cutting
remarks—not *meanness,* but a kind of nervous patter, as if
she fears she might sink into this jostling lunch crowd,
as if by talking sharply she could stay afloat. *He's seating those people*
and I know they got here after us. Where's the other man, this one's
terrible, even your father got into it with him—I cut a glance;
she looks away, dodgy. Dad's been gone six years. Is she—?

Tables *seem* available—we count four—but I'm not sure
how this place operates. I want to lend the benefit of doubt
to everyone. It's appalling how she leads me into suspicion,
but fighting *it* is fighting *her.* This morning in the car
I fingered the tiger-eye beads looped over the rear-view mirror,

drove left-handed while rubbing each bead in turn,
speaking aloud—*I am thankful for the love of my husband,*
I am thankful for my health—a litany of blessings that calmed me,
even when I could think of nothing specific and ticked off bead
after bead, *I am thankful, I am thankful.* Up at six on a Saturday
so Mother and I could go to a quilt show in Lebanon, take lunch
at the Golden Lamb, a 19th-century inn chock-full of Shaker

furniture and "collectibles." We're finally led through a series
of rooms, seated against the wall beside a flock of eight white-
coated doctors. Mother frowns. She tangles me, this woman
who's told so many times the story of false labor on the Fourth
of July, fireworks bursting outside her hospital window, how I refused
to make my entrance for another month. Difficulty: is it just
our natural state? Ours started before I was born.

Lemon Seed Sister

My mother, slicing lemons in the kitchen, gasps and clutches her tummy. Two days later she's home again. The baby does nothing but scream. Her arms and legs covered in fine dark hair. Have you seen her tail, my brother whispers in our shared bedroom, and I believe him. In the creek I hunt for fossils, pretty gravel. Sometimes I find a waxy crawdad shell, its back popped open like a car trunk, the new body inside slipping out so it might continue to grow. Ellen cried so hard, wail after wail until all her breath was squeezed out and she turned purple, a livid prune, shredding the house, the world, by sheer will. I thought she'd die in each horrible interval, refusing the next breath, shutting out the very air. Finally Mom plopped her back in the bassinette, shoved it into the bedroom and shut the door. She'll cry herself to sleep; she has to learn. She asks if I remember, fifty years later at the kitchen table, as blue jays swoop to pluck peanuts she's lined across the deck railing. We watch, count six waiting their turn in the crabapple. I think it might be my fault, she says, worrying toast crumbs with the fork edge into a fresh line. You know. That she's always been so cold.

CUSHION

My sister needs to be the cartilage
between our compound truths: Mom's fallen

twice we know of. We've got to pull out
some furniture. If each of us took a day. She stares

into some space, some place neither
my brother nor I can see—I think Dad is there.

I think the dogs tangle and weave between
his long legs. He's laughing. I think she's not

prepared. Not Mom—*I'm ready, I'm done,*
just sell the house and let them tear it down—but Kay,

the dandelion girl, the one Mark
cuttingly calls *Arts & Entertainment*, who'd rather

bring over movies & popcorn and crash
on Mom's couch than go home to clean

the papers and detritus from her own
kitchen stove. It's too much: the truth of her life's

set aside in her mind, but I can't tell
if her staying here's a fiction, too. Maybe it's just

the only place she can bear to be. What
about after? *One of you,* says Mom, *is going to find*

my body. We glance around the table,
and the look Kay throws, wide-eyed—*Not me*—

shakes my brother to coughing
laughter. As if one could volunteer!

She pushes away from the table,
stomps to the bathroom. *You have to watch out*

for her, says Mom, sotto voce, *She's gonna snap
loose like a balloon*—and I picture again the bursa,

how it can't do its job any longer, the porous
bones of our mother's brittle legs rubbing

together now, the doctor says, *just bone on bone.*

WHERE DOES THE SOUL RESIDE?

She wakes. Gets up to check the locks.
Outside, the stray cat she won't name
has disemboweled a rabbit, drags
the limp carcass under a chair.

Tomorrow, if anyone comes,
she can ask them to sweep the porch
and maybe wash the windows—just
the kitchen. Something's been rubbing

against the glass. Could be raccoons,
or likely that old cat. Someone
dumped it last winter. She's never
fed it. Still, it stays. Wasn't there

a dog? Hers? When? What time is it?
Thick with shadows, the house feels not
exactly lonely, just—ghosted.
The woods press close, a smothering.

Quick as twigsnap, the dream flashes
again to mind: waist deep in brown
water, her father bends to pour
from a coffee can a tiny

blue baby, impossibly small.
His white shirt glows. He turns to her,
shields his mouth with a half-closed fist
the same moment she calls out—

CRY BOX

Because I have no father now, I shudder and break
into tears at the sight of certain old men. Because we moved them

too soon into the larger aquarium, the Tiger Oscars grew
ill, their skin milky then peeling in shreds. Because she endures

unspeakable terrors, my sister fills her house so full
she cannot use the kitchen, the bathroom, her own bed,

and sleeps on my mother's couch. Because I could not save
my lover that long winter, I walked to the cold Susquehanna

but could not enter it. They shivered in distress, large as my
hands, eyes bulging. I stood on the bank, fists jammed

like stones in my pockets, wind hatcheting the river to shards.
When I could stand their suffering no more, I swept them

with the net into a Pyrex bowl, rushed downstairs to dash
them into the snow, and covered them, gasping, with a flat rock.

Because I married a man half my age, I try to limit my weeping
to the shower, a cry box where I ponder how he'll live without me.

WHO ARE YOU?

The space my brother's body made
has filled entirely with smoke. His jacket,
a gray lung, hangs across the long face
of the brown carousel horse behind

our mother's leather sofa. She's fallen
asleep in her chair, her white hair askew,
her head cocked at an alarming angle. He's
stepped off the porch into the dark spongy

yard, training his halogen flashlight
into the trees as if he might silence
the shrilling owl that just won't quit.
Like a man whose throat's been cut

but who keeps on trying to sing. Or nothing
at all like that, though now there's no way
to banish the thought. Just show yourself,
he murmurs. Give me one clean shot.

NOTES

Section epigraphs are from Walt Whitman's "Song of the Open Road."

Footnotes:

"It Was Nothing"
>"Just tall enough to raise the hammer"
>Boyer Rickel, "[a friend confides she chose the flat]",
>from *reliquary*

"Go"
>"All your meals will be in color now."
>Sheila Squillante, "Nouvelle Cuisine Dreams of My Father,"
>from *In This Dream of My Father*

"Dendromancy"
>"The answer always travels slowly."
>Ellen McGrath Smith, "Thou art as tyrannous, so as thou art,"
>from *Lie Low, Goaded Lamb*

"Who Are You?"
>"The space my brother's body made"
>Marie Howe, "The Gate," from *What the Living Do*

About the Author

Ron Mohring is the author of *Survivable World* (The Word Works, 2003 Washington Prize) and of five chapbooks, including *Amateur Grief* (Frank O'Hara Prize) and *The David Museum* (Diagram Chapbook Prize) and, most recently, *Relative Hearts* (Lily Poetry Review). He lives and writes in Cincinnati, Ohio, where he operates Seven Kitchens Press with enduring love.

About The Word Works

Since its founding in 1974, The Word Works has steadily published volumes of contemporary poetry and presented public programs. Its imprints include The Washington Prize, The Tenth Gate Prize, The Hilary Tham Capital Collection, and International Editions.

Monthly, The Word Works offers free programs in its Café Muse Literary Salon. Starting in 2023, the winners of the Jacklyn Potter Young Poets Competition will be presented in the June Café Muse program.

As a 501(c)3 organization, The Word Works has received awards from the National Endowment for the Arts, the National Endowment for the Humanities, the D.C. Commission on the Arts & Humanities, the Witter Bynner Foundation, Poets & Writers, The Writer's Center, Bell Atlantic, the David G. Taft Foundation, and others, including many generous private patrons.

An archive of artistic and administrative materials in the Washington Writing Archive is housed in the George Washington University Gelman Library. The Word Works is a member of the Community of Literary Magazines and Presses and its books are distributed by Small Press Distribution.

wordworksbooks.org

OTHER WORD WORKS BOOKS

Annik Adey-Babinski, *Okay Cool No Smoking Love Pony*
Karren L. Alenier, *From the Belly: Poets Respond to Gerturude Stein's
    Tender Buttons*
Karren L. Alenier, *Wandering on the Outside*
Emily August, *The Punishments Must Be a School*
Jennifer Barber, *The Sliding Boat Our Bodies Made*
Andrea Carter Brown, *September 12*
Willa Carroll, *Nerve Chorus*
Grace Cavalieri, *Creature Comforts* / *The Long Game: Poems Selected & New*
Abby Chew, *A Bear Approaches from the Sky*
Nadia Colburn, *The High Shelf*
Henry Crawford, *The Binary Planet*
Barbara Goldberg, *Berta Broadfoot and Pepin the Short
    / Breaking & Entering: New and Selected Poems*
Akua Lezli Hope, *Them Gone*
Michael Klein, *The Early Minutes of Without: Poems Selected & New*
Deborah Kuan, *Women on the Moon*
Frannie Lindsay, *If Mercy*
Elaine Magarrell, *The Madness of Chefs*
Chloe Martinez, *Ten Thousand Selves*
Marilyn McCabe, *Glass Factory*
JoAnne McFarland, *Identifying the Body*
Leslie McGrath, *Feminists Are Passing from Our Lives*
Kevin McLellan, *Ornitheology*
Ron Mohring, *The Boy Who Reads in the Trees*
A. Molotkov, *Future Symptoms*
Ann Pelletier, *Letter That Never*
W.T. Pfefferle, *My Coolest Shirt*
Ayaz Pirani, *Happy You Are Here*
Robert Sargent, *Aspects of a Southern Story* / *A Woman from Memphis*
Roger Smith, *Radiation Machine Gun Funk*
Jeddie Sophonius, *Love & Sambal*
Julia Story, *Spinster for Hire*
Barbara Ungar, *Naming the Animals*
Cheryl Clark Vermeulen, *They Can Take It Out*
Julie Marie Wade, *Skirted*
Miles Waggener, *Superstition Freeway*
Fritz Ward, *Tsunami Diorama*
Camille-Yvette Welsch, *The Four Ugliest Children in Christendom*
Amber West, *Hen & God*
Maceo Whitaker, *Narco Farm*

www.ingramcontent.com/pod-product-compliance
Lightning Source LLC
Chambersburg PA
CBHW020322090426

42735CB00009B/1367